BEYOND SKIN DEEP

STORIES OF CROSS-CULTURAL ADOPTIONS

PEARL & CHARLES CHIARENZA

with BRITTANEE HERNANDEZ
with WENDY STEPHENSON
with PATRICK MORRISON
with JENNIFER LYNN
with TONYA & MIKE GENEWICK
with CELAINE CHARLES
Edited by MARY GOODEN DIVINE DESTINY PUBLISHING

CONTENTS

FOREWORD

BY JENNIFER LYNN

In a world that increasingly recognizes and celebrates diversity, the experiences of those raised in multicultural households are more relevant than ever. As a Black child adopted by a White family, I have navigated the complexities of identity, belonging, and love. My journey has been shaped by the unique challenges and rich insights that come from growing up in a family that, on the surface, seemed profoundly different from me. Yet, beneath the differences, there was always a foundation of hope.

This book serves as a crucial exploration of multicultural adoption, offering a voice to many who share similar stories. It is a testament to the power of love that transcends race and culture, reminding us that family is defined not only by biology, but by the bonds we create through care, commitment, and understanding.

This project holds special meaning because it is something Matthew deeply wanted to write about. As a biracial adoptee raised in an all-White family, Matt often reflected on both the blessings and the struggles that came with his unique experience. He had a desire to share the good, the hard, and the lessons learned—not just for his own healing, but to support other families walking a similar path. His hope was to offer insight, empathy, and encouragement to adoptees and adoptive families navigating this journey.

For many adoptees, being raised in a different racial or cultural background can lead to a myriad of questions about identity, acceptance, and self-worth. I too, faced these questions. At times, I grappled with the complexities of dual identity, wondering how I fit into a world that often categorizes people by their skin color. But the love I received from my family was a constant reminder that our connections run far deeper than external appearances.

By sharing my story alongside the stories of others, this book aims to illuminate the diverse paths of adoptees in multicultural families. It acknowledges the challenges we face while celebrating the unique perspectives we bring to the table. Through these narratives, we hope to foster understanding, empathy, and awareness of the intricacies of multicultural adoption.

As you read, I invite you to reflect on the power of love that binds families together, regardless of race. The experiences shared within these pages highlight not only the difficulties of navigating cultural differences, but also the profound beauty that emerges when we embrace diversity with open hearts.

To all those touched by adoption, this book is for you. May it inspire conversations, deepen understanding, and ultimately reinforce the truth that love knows no boundaries. Together, we honor the rich tapestry of identities that make up our world and recognize that every story matters.

Reflecting on My Relationship with the Chiarenza Family

The Chiarenza family is a beautiful tapestry of love, hope, and resilience that has profoundly impacted my life. I first met Pearl four years ago when she reached out for my photography services for her Empowering Women's Retreat. It was a transformative experience, not just for the participants but for me as well, as I witnessed the strength and inspiration Pearl brings to her community.

A couple of years later, Pearl asked me to capture their family portraits. Little did we know this would be their last family photo session before the tragic passing of her son, Matthew. It was a day filled with bittersweet emotion. We were there to celebrate Nathaniel's college graduation, a milestone that brought joy and pride to the family.

During that session, I was moved by Matthew's quiet grace. He was a true gentleman, a gentle soul. I watched him assist his father and grandmother, guiding them with compassion and love. Though he spoke little, his actions communicated volumes—revealing the depth of his character and the warmth of his heart.

Matthew's life was cut far too short, yet his spirit endures in the memories we cherish and the stories we continue to share. Through the beautiful moments captured in photographs, and in the love and laughter preserved in those memories, we honor Matthew and the life he lived.

As I reflect on my relationship with the Chiarenza family, I am reminded of the power of connection, the strength of community, and the deep love that binds us together. Their resilience in the face of loss is a profound testament to the strength of family. I feel grateful to have been part of their journey.

Matthew's memory will continue to inspire us, reminding us to embrace each moment and celebrate the lives we hold dear.

1

PEARL AND CHARLES CHIARENZA

A JOURNEY OF LOVE AND FAMILY

Adopting our son Matthew was a journey that began with hope and a deep longing to start a family. After over a decade of struggling to have a child, my husband Chuck and I turned to Catholic Charities, believing that their thorough background checks and dedication would help us find the perfect match. Yet, as we navigated the process, we quickly realized it wasn't the right fit for us. The interviews were lengthy and invasive, and at one point, my own parents were questioned about things like whether Chuck had a drinking problem, simply because we had beer in our basement fridge. This, along with the intense focus on Chuck's past grief over losing family members, made us question whether this was truly the path we were meant to take.

Feeling uncertain, we stepped away from Catholic Charities, unsure of what the future would hold. Then, a twist of fate came when Chuck's mother visited a psychic who predicted that she would become a grandmother by the end of the year. Although we initially laughed it off, life had other plans. A few months later, we received a call about a baby boy who needed a loving home. Within two weeks, we made the decision to adopt him, and though we had concerns about how our family and friends might react to having a mixed-race child, we knew in our hearts that Matthew was meant to be ours.

Bringing Matthew Home and Growing Our Family

Our journey to bring Matthew home was both interesting and challenging. In California, the adoption process was finalized within 24 hours, allowing us to welcome Matthew into our lives almost immediately. However, returning to Virginia required an interstate adoption process that soon became overwhelming and frustrating. Despite completing all the paperwork, we were constantly told that more documentation was needed. After about a month of delays, I finally decided that enough was enough and set a firm date for our return home, regardless of the lingering bureaucracy.

When we finally arrived back in Virginia with Matthew, it felt like the beginning of a beautiful new chapter in our lives. At that time, we were simply overjoyed to be parents to this wonderful boy and weren't yet facing the complexities of raising a child of a different culture.

Two years later, we decided to grow our family again. After a few attempts at in vitro fertilization and some setbacks, our fertility clinic offered us a new procedure at no additional cost. We decided this would be our final attempt before considering adoption once more. That final attempt brought us our second beautiful bundle of joy, our son Nathaniel, who was born in 2000.

When we brought Nathaniel home, it sparked the first real conversation about race within our family. Matthew, who was almost three at the time, no longer a toddler, asked us why his baby brother was a different color than he was. We explained as simply as we could that his heritage was a blend of Czechoslovakian and Haitian backgrounds, which made him who he was, and that Nathaniel's heritage was German and Italian, which made him who he was. This conversation made us realize the importance of connecting with other adoptive families and seeking out support and community to help us navigate these questions as they arose.

Nathaniel, at about two and a half years old, he had his own moment of recognition regarding race. As a baby, Nathaniel often scratched his arms, and we weren't sure why. We considered consulting a doctor to see if it was a behavioral concern. Then, one winter day, after playing outside in the snow with his friends, Nathaniel came inside, crying uncontrollably and scratching at his arms. I took off his coat, sat him down, and gently asked him what was wrong. Through his tears, he said, "I want to be like brother," believing that he could scratch his skin to become the same color as Matthew. At that moment, we realized it was time to have the same conversation with Nathaniel that we had once had with Matthew. We explained that his unique heritage was what made him special, and that our differences were what made our family beautifully unique.

A New Chapter in Florida: Navigating Challenges and Growth

When Matthew was in fourth grade and Nathaniel in first, our family made the decision to move to Florida. We hoped that this move would offer Matthew more cultural exposure and a sense of belonging. However, we later realized that we hadn't fully anticipated some of the challenges that would come with this transition.

As Matthew entered middle school, he began to face difficulties with peers who noticed that he was a different race from his family. Unfortunately, this led to bullying and made it challenging for him to find his place of belonging. This was also around the time when *The Blind Side* movie came out, and it resonated deeply with our family as we tried to understand Matthew's experiences and emotions.

In his search for a sense of belonging, Matthew sometimes connected with peers who were also struggling, and this didn't always lead to the best choices. We decided to enroll him in a school program called AVID (a college readiness program) to help him find a supportive community and peers who looked like him. As he moved into high school, Matthew joined the football team, which he had always loved since playing peewee football, but he continued to face challenges related to his identity.

In his junior year of high school, we decided it might be time to explore more about his birth family. We had stayed in contact with his birth mom, and Matthew remembered meeting her when he was younger. One day, through Facebook, we found one of her friends who looked remarkably like Matthew, and we believed in our hearts that he was Matthew's birth father. After consulting with Matthew's therapist, we decided to approach his birth mom for more information, but the meeting left us with more questions than answers.

When we met with Matthew's birth mom, we hoped to gain clarity, but instead, we encountered different stories than the ones we had been told when we adopted him. The name she provided for his birth father was different, and the details of his birth varied. As we left, I apologized to Matthew, feeling like we hadn't found the answers he was seeking. But he reassured me, saying that he believed the answers we had discovered were accurate. He had done his own research and knew that the name his birth mom gave was his birth father's legal name, not the nickname he used as an NFL player and scout. This moment of reassurance was a testament to Matthew's resilience and determination to understand his own story.

Navigating Adulthood: Challenges, Growth, and Healing

As Matthew transitioned into adulthood, the journey was filled with moments of self-discovery, struggles, and growth. After the meeting with his birth mom, we returned home with a mix of emotions. While we had hoped it would bring clarity, it ultimately shaped Matthew's reflections and mental fitness in ways we hadn't anticipated.

One of the challenging aspects was how Mother's Day became a complex time for us. Matthew often struggled with how to label his feelings: I was his mom, the one who was always there, while his birth mom was the person who gave him life. It took time, but he eventually shared that he saw me as the steady presence in his life, Mom, while his birth mom, Mother, remained a figure tied to his origins, despite the inconsistency in her stories.

As Matthew entered college, starting in Kentucky and then transferring to a school in Florida, we discovered that he had been drinking more heavily than we realized. College life, combined with the lingering sense of not fully belonging, influenced some of his choices, and it became clear that he was struggling with mental health challenges. This period also impacted his relationship with his brother Nate, as Matthew's struggles often took center stage, creating challenges for the entire family.

It was during this time that in his quest for belonging, Matthew also chose to join the army. We were hopeful that this path would offer him the structure and camaraderie he sought. However, he realized that it wasn't the right fit for him, leading to his discharge after struggling with physical requirements. He came home, but soon after his drinking and mental thinking was a struggle.

In seeking help, Matthew made the courageous decision to go to rehab. The first facility was not the best choice, as it was more focused on money, rather than therapy and accountability. When Matthew did not adhere to their contract we set, we made the incredibly difficult decision to ask him to leave our home. This was the hardest decision. Shortly after this, he got his first DUI and made an attempt to take his life. His brother Nate was with us that day and helped Matthew see his life was worthy. Matt never forgot that.

He was doing better, but the drinking was still an issue. Around this time, he connected with a group of young Black men, and he felt a sense of belonging. This happened during the time we were having counseling sessions with his amazing therapist, Rachel. She would see Matthew one week and meet with us as a family unit the next.

Unfortunately, this group introduced him to some disturbing religious beliefs. According to their teachings, as White people, we were not recognized in the Bible and were doomed because we were not made of the color of dirt. They believed our time on Earth was limited.

It was terrifying. We didn't know how to navigate this with Matthew.

I remember reaching out to a friend, a Black man very connected in faith, for guidance. He had shared that they had lost three Black boys from their church to similar ideologies. He advised us to simply ask Matthew, "How can we support you in these thoughts?", this was very hard.

During one therapy session, Matthew told us that because of our faith we were doomed, and he was worried that he might be the one who would have to "skin" us. This was the belief they had influenced him to believe. We knew they were a cult. All I could say in that session was, "Matthew, how can we support you in your thoughts?", and "I believe that God knows when and how we will leave this Earth, and if that is how we are to go, it would sadden me, but I know we will be with God!" Matthew sat back not knowing what to say, and then he said his stomach hurt and he had to leave. I believe this was a turning point. A few months later, during the tail end of COVID he decided to go to Texas for rehab. By the grace of God, we received financial help and were able to send him there.

His real work started on mental health—recognizing that he was involved in a cult, understanding that his negative words during Mother's Day activities made me feel less worthy and how his behavior affected his relationship with his brother.

Matt came home from rehab in July of 2021 with a new outlook and a commitment to continuing his counseling with Rachel.

A Journey of Hope and Heartache

When Matthew came home from his second stay in rehab, it felt like a new chapter was beginning. His relationship with Brittanee brought a sense of purpose and joy into his life, and he embraced Brittanee's daughter as if she were his own. On the surface, things seemed to be falling into place. They were building a life together, and he was helping out with the business he and his dad had started. There was hope and optimism, but beneath that, we knew Matthew was still grappling with inner struggles.

By early 2022, some of those challenges resurfaced. Although Matthew had reduced his drinking, it remained a struggle as he continued to work through the emotional complexities of his adoption and his identity.

Matthew and Brittanee moved in together, and it seemed like they were on a path toward a future as a family. He still saw his therapist, Rachel, and while there were moments of progress, we knew that healing is never a linear journey. There were ups and downs, and we held on to hope.

As July 2022 approached, just after Matthew's 25th birthday, a disagreement with Brittanee led to a difficult day. Instead of working through his emotions or coming home, Matthew turned to drinking again. That night, he made the heart-breaking decision to drive, and in a tragic accident, we lost him.

As we grappled with the overwhelming grief of losing Matthew, we also faced another harsh reality. When we discovered his passing through a news report rather than a direct notification. It became clear that assumptions had been made. Because Matthew had a DUI in his past and alcohol was found at the scene, it seemed that those in charge of notifying us didn't see the urgency in reaching out. This lack of immediate communication made us feel that Matthew wasn't given the dignity and respect he deserved, and it highlighted the presence of bias even in the most tragic of moments. While Matthew made a mistake that night, he still deserved to be treated with compassion, and we hope that by sharing his story, we can help ensure that no other family experiences such a painful oversight.

Matthew's Legacy: A Message of Love, Awareness, and Inclusion

In sharing Matthew's story, we honor his legacy and the vision he held for a world where love and understanding transcend all differences. Matthew faced many challenges, including the racism he experienced from his grandfather and the lack of honesty from his birth mother about his birth father. When we reached out to the man, we believed to be his birth dad, we were met with avoidance and ultimately no closure, leaving lingering questions. Even in his passing, reaching out to his birth parents brought a stark reminder of the emotional complexities and the importance of genuine connection.

Yet, through these challenges, we remain steadfast in our belief that adoption is a beautiful and transformative journey. This book is not only a tribute to Matthew's life but also a call to action for families to open their hearts to adoption. It's a reminder that when adopting a child of a different culture, it's essential to build a supportive and inclusive community. Embracing their cultural heritage, asking the right questions, and ensuring they feel seen and valued are all crucial parts of the journey.

The Big Schemer and His Dad – A Father's Thoughts

My oldest son, Matthew, was a magnet that drew adults and children to him. He brought positive energy to any room he entered. He easily started conversations with friends and strangers alike. He had a strong-willed determination when he set his mind to something. It was a joy to watch when he was focused on a goal. But truth be told, it could also be frustrating—within four to six months of diving headfirst into something, he often lost interest and moved on to the next passion.

His longest-lasting passion was football. He begged, pleaded, and threw more than a few tantrums until we finally agreed to let him play Pop Warner football. After just two practices, he was hooked. Football became his world. He dreamed of playing in the NFL, and he chased that dream with everything he had. That passion stayed strong through high school and into the start of his college playing days. When he lost the spark near the end of his first season, it hit him hard—and it hit me hard, too. I'd seen how much joy it brought him. Watching that dream fade was tough for both of us.

Matthew was also a classic teenage schemer—always up to something. He often butted heads with his mom, especially when she caught him doing things he wasn't supposed to. Like the time he tried to keep a snake in his room. Those two could argue for days about that snake and everything else he tried to sneak past us. That's how he earned his nicknames: *The Big Schemer* and *Whinny B*—names that still make me smile.

He was fiercely loyal. He loved his brother, his mother, and me deeply. He was usually full of energy and opinions. He'd debate just about anything for the fun of it. But there were also times—especially when he had too much to drink—when the mood would shift. He could fall into a place of negativity, even depression. Those moments gave us glimpses of deeper struggles he didn't always know how to talk about.

One of the most painful things to witness as his father was watching him try to navigate the challenges of being biracial in a family and community that didn't always reflect who he was. While we loved him completely, I look back now and realize there were moments we simply didn't understand what he needed most. There were conversations I wish we had earlier. Guidance I wish I could have given. I didn't fully recognize how much he longed to see himself reflected in the world around him, in places like our church, our friend groups, or even in our extended family.

I know he felt hurt when certain family members—like my father-n-law, who wouldn't see past the color of his skin. As a dad, that's something I carry with me. I didn't fully understand just how deep those wounds could go until later. I'd give anything to go back and do more to shield him from that, or to stand beside him more boldly when he needed it most.

Still, Matthew found joy. He built lasting friendships, many of which started back in middle and high school. Our house was always full of his friends—laughing, wrestling, gaming, competing. It was loud, chaotic, and full of life. Those nights filled my heart with joy.

Later, he built something special with Brittanee and her daughter. Seeing him take pride in being part of their little family gave me hope that he had found his place—his home. He showed a kind of tenderness and maturity that made me incredibly proud. Watching him with them gave me peace, even as he continued to wrestle with his identity and his past.

If there's one thing I hope others take from Matthew's story, it's this: love your children deeply —but don't stop there. Learn what they need that you might not see. Ask hard questions. Make sure they don't just feel loved, but understood. Especially if they're growing up in a world where they feel different. If I could say one more thing to my son, it would be this: *You were enough. Always.*

Matthew's Enduring Gift

Nate, in his beautiful eulogy for Matthew, reminded us of the deep bond they shared. Despite the struggles, their love for one another was unwavering. One of the greatest gifts Matthew left behind is the legacy of his relationship with Brittanee and her daughter. They are now a permanent part of our family, with Brittanee as our daughter-in-love and her daughter as our granddaughter. Their presence is a testament to the enduring love and the beautiful connections that continue to grow from Matthew's life.

As we remember Matthew, we hold on to the belief that everyone deserves to be loved and that we are all equal in that love. May Matthew's story inspire others to open their hearts, embrace diversity, and create a world where every child feels a true sense of belonging.

2

BRITTANEE HERNANDEZ

FROM TWIN FLAMES TO GUARDIAN WINGS

Matthew and I were more alike than I can ever express—we were like twins, constantly finishing each other's sentences and reading each other's minds. In so many ways, we were mirrors of one another. We could talk and laugh for hours, about anything and everything.

We met on a dating app, both guarded from past experiences. We had been hurt before, and trust didn't come easily. But we took our time and let our connection unfold naturally. Eventually, we moved in together, and it felt like the beginning of a beautiful chapter. Matthew was so attentive, present, and passionate about our bond. I had high hopes for the family we were building together. From our long talks, I understood Matthew's struggles, and I believed in him. I believed that with my love and gentle nature, I could help him through anything. He was worth it.

Matthew had a beautifully complex mind, filled with knowledge and curiosity. He was an incredible storyteller—I could sit and listen to him talk for hours, whether he was sharing the latest from his favorite podcast, his research of the day, or simply recounting his thoughts. He was brilliant, articulate, and deeply thoughtful. Together, we made a strong team—what I lacked, he offered; what he needed, I could give. We respected and understood each other deeply.

One of the things I cherished most about Matthew was his openness. When he trusted someone, he invited them into his inner world without reservation. I always met that vulnerability with compassion and grace. Though he had so much going for him outwardly, Matthew carried emotional wounds rooted in cultural displacement and unanswered questions about his birth family.

We dreamed of traveling to Haiti and the Czech Republic, hoping that connecting with his homelands would help him feel grounded in his identity. He often spoke about how meaningful it would be to stand on the soil of his ancestors, to finally feel a sense of belonging.

We also made plans to meet his birth mother, who, by coincidence, lived in the same state as my brother. It felt like the universe was aligning things for us. Our vision was simple—no cameras, no pressure, just a face-to-face conversation, heart to heart, free of judgment. They had exchanged text messages from time to time, and he would always share them with me. She seemed kind but lost, a woman burdened by her own past, unable to offer the clarity Matthew desperately needed. Still, even with the pain her silence caused, Matthew showed her grace.

Sometimes, when he drank, those feelings would rise to the surface—he'd bring up her messages, revisit the confusion, the longing, the hurt. Despite all of it, he never harbored anger, just pain and indifference. We both hoped that visiting her together might give him some sense of peace. I truly believed that, with support, the right questions, and open hearts, we might find healing and closure.

Matthew lived a life full of adventure, passion, and potential. He was deeply involved in MMA, which gave him a strong sense of purpose and community. He was training hard, had fights lined up, and we were even setting up a home workout space in our shed. But when an issue forced him to leave his gym, it shattered his sense of belonging and spiraled him into a dark place. At times, Matthew struggled with alcohol—not as a constant presence, but when he did drink, it brought his inner pain to the surface. Still, I remained his light, meeting him with love, patience, and peace. I truly believed we could weather any storm together.

When he lost his gym, he poured himself into a new dream: starting a puppy kennel. He loved animals deeply and had a natural connection with them. After he passed, the puppies we brought home went to loving homes—close friends who could carry a piece of Matthew's heart with them. He was always trying to rescue animals, even stopping in traffic to save a turtle. He was a gentle giant, an animal whisperer.

For his birthday in 2022, his parents offered to watch Evey so we could go out. Matthew could have picked a bar or a restaurant—but instead, he chose a family outing to the aquarium. That was who he was: a man who valued family above all. He and Evey shared a beautiful bond. She's very reserved and slow to warm up, but Matthew won her heart. They played video games together, and he was her big teddy bear. He had endless patience and love for her. He was so excited about fatherhood and took his role seriously. I couldn't have asked for a more devoted partner.

We had so many dreams. He missed Virginia, and we hoped to buy a cabin there one day. We had business plans, travel dreams, and even considered fostering children shortly before his passing. We had completed the application process and were waiting for more information. Matthew's only request was that the child resemble us to avoid teasing, which broke my heart—he just wanted everyone to feel like they belonged.

Matthew loved thrifting. He once came home with a gift bag full of sunflower-themed treasures just for me, knowing how much I loved them. He once found me a gorgeous thrifted easel with drawers, knowing how much I loved art. It's one of my most cherished memories.

Matthew's passing was not due to lack of love or support—his family never turned their back on him. They were always there, even when he struggled. His battles were within, tied to a longing for identity and cultural connection. He knew he had a good life, but his heart ached for a deeper understanding of self. For some, those feelings pass. For Matthew, they never truly left. He wore his heart on his sleeve and just wanted to belong.

His loss is a tragedy—he was a radiant soul with a warrior's heart. His smile lit up the room. His voice lit up mine. He is now our guardian angel, and I know he's still watching over us. While grief comes in waves, and the pain never fully fades, I find peace knowing he is near. I'll forever be grateful for the love we shared.

> *"It is better to have loved and lost than never to have loved at all"* — Alfred Lord Tennyson.

I was blessed beyond words to love Matthew.

3

WENDY STEPHENSON

A FAMILY KNIT ACROSS CONTINENTS

There are moments in life that stretch your heart wider than you ever knew it could go. For us, one of those moments was stepping out of the van at a small orphanage in Sierra Leone, greeted by the sound of children singing songs of welcome. As they performed a simple ceremony to honor our arrival, my eyes scanned the crowd—and then found his. Mo. In the middle of the group, his eyes met mine, and I saw them light up. In that moment, something eternal passed between us. It was the beginning of a bond that no paperwork or passport stamp could ever define. We weren't just adding to our family—we were expanding our understanding of love, identity, and the beauty of diversity.

Our adoption journey began not with a perfect plan, but with a stirring. A holy nudge. At the time, we had three biological children. Life was full, but there was a deeper call—a whisper from the Lord that there was more. When we first traveled to Sierra Leone, we had no idea that we'd return home not only with three children in our hearts but also a fourth growing in my womb. Our youngest biological daughter was born between our first trip and the homecoming of our adoptive children. God's timing is never accidental.

We adopted Abubakarr (17), Mohamed (13), and Esther (6). Esther had been abandoned by her parents and left on the streets of Sierra Leone due to her disability. Abu and Mo had a living mother we believed wasn't involved, only to later discover she was. That revelation brought its own complexity, grief, and reckoning

From the beginning, we knew this journey wasn't just about adding names to our family tree—it was about weaving lives, cultures, and stories together. We didn't want our children to erase who they were to fit into our life. We wanted to build a life that held space for all of us to be fully known and fully seen.

We celebrate African Child's Day and the anniversary of their arrival with Sierra Leonean dishes and joy. These aren't just meals—they're moments of remembrance and honor. A way of saying: we see where you came from, and it matters deeply.

But this path hasn't been without its heartbreak. We walked through language barriers, cultural misfires, trauma triggers, and deep emotional valleys. We had to learn how to parent differently—through the lens of grief, loss, and rebuilding trust. It wasn't just about consistency; it was about compassion. And sometimes, the most Christlike thing we could do was to listen more than we spoke.

One of the hardest parts of our journey was what unfolded with Abu. Despite our deepest efforts, there came a time—after he turned eighteen—when the safety of our family was at risk due to his behavior and violent threats. We made the incredibly painful decision to release him from our home. It's a grief we still carry, and yet, we trust God with his life and healing. Not every story ties up with a neat bow—but every child deserves to be safe, and so does every other member of the family.

And then there's Esther. Sweet, radiant Esther. Her story is different from the boys'. Born with cerebral palsy and abandoned on the streets of Sierra Leone, her life hung in the balance when we met her. By the time she arrived in the U.S., she was on the verge of starvation and was immediately hospitalized at Vanderbilt. The doctors determined she needed a feeding tube to restore basic nutrition. It was one of the most sobering moments of our journey—realizing that had she not come home with us when she did, she likely wouldn't be alive today.

Esther is nonverbal and uses a wheelchair full-time. Our days are filled with therapies, specialist visits, and complex care routines—but they're also filled with her laughter. She loves watching her siblings play, belly laughs at silly noises, and insists on listening to African music at full blast. She brings joy into every room without ever saying a word. Her life is not defined by what she cannot do, but by the light she carries. In her own quiet way, Esther teaches us daily what resilience, joy, and unconditional love really look like.

Mohamed, on the other hand, hasn't simply *fit in*—he's left his signature everywhere he walks. His high school football coach pulled me aside once and said, "Mo is the most impactful and positive student I've met in my lifetime of teaching and coaching." That light has opened doors: athlete of the year, a football scholarship to college, and a campus wide reputation for kindness that outshines his stat sheet. He holds doors, mentors freshmen, and ends every practice with a grin that reminds everyone why the game matters. Watching him step into who he is with confidence and humility has been one of the richest gifts of our journey.

We couldn't have done this alone. Early on, we found a circle of families who also adopted from Sierra Leone. That group became more than a support network—they became a lifeline. They helped us navigate everything from paperwork to the quiet ache of not always getting it right. They reminded us that we weren't alone, and neither were our kids.

The journey of adoption doesn't end at homecoming—it continues in every conversation, every misunderstanding, every victory. It's in the awkward moments and the sweet ones. It's in the decisions we make to keep showing up, even when we feel inadequate.

We've also had intentional conversations about race, color, and culture. Mo's first culture is Sierra Leonean, and his native language is Krio—he still chats with friends back home almost daily. Because he didn't grow up inside American racial dynamics, he carries a lightness many Black Americans aren't afforded. Yet I've had to prepare him for the reality that some people here *will* judge him by what they think they see. Simple things—like pulling a hood low on a chilly night—can be misread. So, I taught him what my dad called "eyes up, chin high": make eye contact, let your joy speak first, and never dim your light to make others comfortable.

Still, we celebrate the fullness of his identity: Tennessee twang layered over Krio slang, faith soaked in Sierra Leonean rhythm. He dreams of returning one day to help families in Freetown keep their children despite poverty's pull. His vision reminds me that our goal was never assimilation; it was *activation*—releasing each child to change the world in their own God-given way.

To any family considering cross-cultural adoption, I offer this:

- Don't do it to be the hero. Do it to be a student of someone else's story.
- Be prepared to let go of your expectations. Adoption will break you open—in the best and hardest ways.
- Don't erase their past. Let it live on in your present.
- Surround yourself with people who understand. You need community, and so do your kids.
- Don't just love them. Learn who they are.

Adoption is a calling. It is beautiful. It is brutal. It is beyond skin deep.

As I look around my home today—a mix of Tennessee roots and Sierra Leonean spirit—I see redemption in motion. Not because everything turned out how we imagined, but because God's grace held us through the parts we never could have predicted.

This isn't the end of the story. It's just one chapter—one filled with beauty, breaking, and belonging. The kind of chapter that shapes the rest of the book.

I've learned that love isn't a strategy. It's a sacrifice. And when you choose to step into a child's world, culture and all, you aren't just offering them a family—you're giving them the dignity of being fully seen and fully known.

Our family has been stretched, refined, and ultimately strengthened through this journey. We are not perfect, but we are present. We do not have all the answers, but we serve a God who sees every detail and redeems every broken place.

To the mother wondering if she can love a child who doesn't share her history—yes, you can. And when you do, you'll discover how much they have to teach you.

To the father worried about navigating unfamiliar traditions or languages—stay curious. Stay humble. The goal is not to replace their past but to build something beautiful with it.

And to the child who feels torn between two worlds

—know this: you are not in between. You are both. And you belong.

Our story continues—through college phone calls, Krio phrases shouted from the kitchen, late-night conversations, and quiet prayers for a son who's no longer under our roof but never outside of God's reach.

This journey has taken us beyond skin deep. And for that, I am forever grateful.

4

PATRICK MORRISON

HOW I BECAME A MORRISON—AND RUINED MY BAPTISM OUTFIT

AN ORIGIN STORY

In the late ’80s, Easter Sunday was a pastel fever dream. Big hair, bigger shoulder pads, and the kind of family photos where everyone looked like they’d been styled by a JC Penney catalog and a can of Aquanet.

That particular Easter, my future family—Terri and Nick Morrison and my soon-to-be sisters, Kelly and Briana—were driving out to Mesa, Arizona to spend the day at Grandma’s house. The girls, eight and six, were stuffed into scratchy dresses with lace collars and sat stiffly in the back seat, trying not to wrinkle anything important.

They pulled up to Grandma’s like they always did: through the garage. This was a suburban ritual. Cars were guided with precision thanks to a tennis ball suspended from the ceiling, dangling just low enough to tap the windshield when you'd gone far enough in. A low-tech guidance system, courtesy of Grandpa Engineering.

Inside, the smell of Easter dinner hung in the air—turkey, mashed potatoes, soft dinner rolls, and gravy with that perfect skin forming on top. And of course, the can-shaped cranberry sauce on a plate, ridges intact. That was my dad's favorite.

And then the day took a turn.

Right in the middle of dinner prep, a man walked in —unannounced, very much in his Easter best—and popped the cork on a champagne bottle.

"It's a boy!" he shouted.

Now, nobody in the room was pregnant. The announcement wasn't meant for Grandma. It was for Terri and Nick, my future parents.

Because in a hospital across the border in Mexicali, Mexico, I had just been born.

A premature baby with jaundice and a future full of neglecting sunscreen, I entered the world just in time to crash Easter dinner—metaphorically—for a family that had been trying to adopt for years.

The man with the champagne? That was Manny, my dad's business partner at the time. Years earlier, he and my father had invested in a hospital in Mexicali, run by a mutual friend. And on that day, the network of dads, deals, and divine timing all clicked into place. Someone at the hospital knew the Morrisons were looking to adopt, and as luck—or grace—would have it, a baby had just been born and was being placed for adoption.

An Easter miracle.

It's not your typical adoption story, but nothing about my arrival was typical. My future parents had already experienced a few heartbreaking adoption near-misses—connections that fell through, adoptions that unraveled at the last minute. They were on an emotional rollercoaster of hope and heartbreak.

But this time, something felt different.

Manny gave them the news, and my mom said her heart stopped. They didn't even finish dinner. The next morning, Terri, Nick, and Briana packed the car and headed south to the border. Kelly, the oldest, had to stay behind for standardized testing—which, if you think about it, is a cruel cosmic joke. What eight-year-old wants to be stuck filling in Scantron bubbles while the rest of her family drives off to meet their new baby brother?

I teased her about it over the years. In hindsight, I realize how hard that must've been. I know she wanted to be there.

Sorry, Kelly. Sibling rivalry is inevitable—but that one might have crossed a line.

When my family arrived in Mexicali, they were greeted by family friends—one of whom held a bundle wrapped in what would become known in Morrison lore as The Blue Blanket.

That blanket was legendary. It shows up again and again in our photo albums—faded, pilled, worn soft over time. But in that first moment, it was pristine. And inside it, *me*.

My mom told me that the second she saw me, her heart dropped into her chest in the best possible way. That breathless, tearful "this is it" kind of moment. When they placed me in her arms, she knew instantly, I was her son. No hesitation. Just a click, like a key in a lock.

She was a nurse, and when she looked at me, she saw a tiny, fragile newborn who needed love—and probably sunlight. I was so small my dad says he could hold me across one palm. And jaundiced. When my mom asked where the blue light machine was, like the hospital she worked at, someone pointed outside and said, "Just hold him in the sun."

Before I could leave the country, there was one stipulation: I had to be baptized in the Catholic Church. My mom, a Catholic herself, didn't hesitate. She would've walked through fire to bring me home.

So the big day arrived. My mom dressed me in a beautiful white baptismal outfit—crisp, delicate, angelic. She was beaming. Proud. Running on adrenaline and reapplying her red lipstick careful not to get it on her teeth. The Morrison family was ready.

And then, according to her vivid (and frequently repeated) retelling, I exploded.

It wasn't subtle. She describes it as *violent diarrhea.* All over the white garment. With minutes to spare before the ceremony, she rushed me to the church parking lot and performed a triage-level wardrobe change in the back seat of the car.

The backup outfit? Let's just say it lacked reverence but made up for it in symbolism. I like to imagine it was one of my dad's old race T-shirts—something oversized with "Triathlon Finisher" or "Tucson Marathon Runner" plastered across it. I know it probably wasn't that dramatic. But I also know my mom wasn't going to allow her poop-ridden newborn to be baptized in soiled robes.

Still, I made it to the altar. Sweaty. Slightly underdressed. Holy water was poured. Blessings were said. I became a Morrison in the eyes of the Catholic Church.

Now came the real challenge: getting a Mexican-born baby across the U.S. border.

They wrapped me back in the blue blanket, packed up the car, and headed toward the checkpoint. My parents were nervous. You don't just drive up in a Mercedes with a brown baby and expect zero questions.

Their plan? Act natural. Hope I stayed asleep. And say they didn't buy anything.

They pulled up to the gate. The officer leaned in. My dad gripped the steering wheel. My mom tried not to sweat and Briana stayed quiet n the backseat.

"Did you buy anything?" the officer asked.

A pause.

"No," my dad said.

The officer nodded. "Alright. Have a good day."

And that was it. No inspection. No baby-related follow-up questions.

Just like that, I crossed into the United States—wrapped in a blue blanket, asleep in the backseat, freshly baptized, at that moment my journey as a Morrison began.

We still have that blue blanket. It's worn thin now, fraying at the edges. But to my mom, it's sacred. To me, it's proof—that the moment she saw me, something clicked for both of us.

People sometimes ask if I've ever wanted to find my birth mother. And I've thought about it. It would be to thank her for making that sacrifice. For me to have a better chance at a good life. But what I always return to is this: I never felt like I was missing anything. Not because I wasn't curious, but because I never felt out of place in my family.

My story began in Mexicali. But it came alive the moment a woman held a tiny baby wrapped in a blue blanket and said, "This is my son."

It wasn't a perfect start. There was chaos. There was paperwork. There was poop on a baptism gown.

But if that's not family, I don't know what is.

Final Thoughts

When I think about the lengths my parents and family went through just to get me, I'm reminded of the love, dedication, and courage it took to bring me into their lives. It was a choice they made—a choice that's always made me feel special.

My family chose me.

And I've learned that true love isn't some grand, cinematic gesture. It's a daily act. A quiet commitment. A choice we make again and again. When I think of love, it's impossible to separate that feeling from my idea of family. The two are fused together.

People sometimes ask me what it's like being adopted. My knee-jerk response?

"I'm a lottery winner."

Because that's what it feels like. I won the lottery with my family.

That doesn't mean everything has been perfect. We've had our share of struggles and arguments—some petty, like fighting over the front seat, and others deeper. I've wrestled with my identity. Wondered where I fit in.

As a kid, it wasn't always easy being the brown one in a white family. I saw the looks people gave us. I heard the questions. "Who are your real parents?"

Sometimes I wished I could just look like the rest of my family—because maybe then people wouldn't stare. Maybe they'd believe my sisters were really my sisters.

But it's through those uncomfortable moments, the

weird questions, the awkward silences—that my family and I grew closer.

Because family isn't about matching genetics. It's about the people who choose you, show up for you, and love you through everything, even. Even the *violent diarrhea in a Mexican church parking lot* kind of moments.

And if you ask me whether I'd trade my story for an easier one, the answer is no.

I am a Morrison.

And I'm the luckiest lottery winner I know.

5

JENNIFER LYNN

A PLACE BETWEEN TWO WORLDS

I was five days old when I was placed into the arms of my adoptive parents. Born from a Black father and a white mother, I was part of a world in the late 1970s that had not yet embraced African-American mixed children. The color of my skin made it difficult for family adoption placement at first, but the adoption agency was eventually able to find a family fit for me.

God had a plan for my life. A scripture I have always stuck by is:

> *"For I know the plans I have for you,' declares the Lord, 'plans to prosper you and not to harm you, plans to give you hope and a future.'"*—Jeremiah 29:11 (NIV)

It was confusing internally growing up between two worlds regarding my Identity. Especially as a Black child with Caucasian adoptive parents. My parents were charitable. Even though they did not fully understand the complexities of my cultural background or what it meant for a mixed girl growing up in a predominantly White environment.

They assisted with my daily needs and I am grateful for that.

Yet their love was in question. There were teachings they were yet to learn, lessons that would be crucial in shaping my sense of self. I was raised in a Catholic religious household.

The Catholic religion spoke of God, yet did not teach direct relationship with God. Even as a little girl, I always knew God. I would speak and hear from Him often. God showed me my birth mother was a broken woman, and she did not have the capacity or capabilities to raise me. I would later find out that she was 19 years old with a 9th grade education when she delivered me.

She didn't find out that she was pregnant with me until she was seven months pregnant. It was too late for her to abort me, therefore, she carried out the pregnancy.

I believe this was God. If she had found out any sooner, she may have aborted me. I am grateful to God and my mother for life. I have God's Holy Spirit in me.

I believe my adopted parents were taught religion through Catholicism, not a relationship with God's Holy Spirit. This may have been the main reason they did not understand me.

The Family I Was Given

When I was adopted, I was welcomed into a multicultural home. My adoptive mother had always desired children but was unable to have her own. She and my adoptive father chose to build a family in an unconventional way, through adoption. There were eight of us altogether: two African American brothers, four Caucasian brothers, one Asian sister and then me. My parents never once treated our racial backgrounds as a barrier, but instead celebrated the fact that they had a diverse family, one that defied societal expectations and traditional norms.

Though our household was full of children from different backgrounds, the focus was always on togetherness. Our family was considered diverse for the 1970's, which meant we were often subject to silent judgment from the outside world. But inside our home race wasn't the defining factor of who we were. We were simply brothers and sisters, sharing the same dinner table, the same family memories, and the same family trips.

Our family was rooted in religion. We were raised in a Catholic household where Jesus was mentioned, yet not personally known. Speaking about Him and truly knowing Him are very different things.

We were taught to volunteer our time and to assist others, putting others' needs before our own. One Bible verse that supports this teaching is:

> *"Let each of you look not only to his own interests, but also to the interests of others."*—Philippians 2:4 (ESV)

This teaching laid a foundation for prioritizing others regardless of the color of their skin. I appreciate this teaching.

Exploring My Identity

Despite the assistance from my family, being a Black child in a Caucasian family was difficult, both inside and outside of our home. I attended a predominantly White school, And because there were only a few Black kids there, I was left curious about my culture.

I was fortunate to have an African American physical education teacher who mentored me. She was a huge blessing during my childhood years–praise God. She spent time with me and educated me on my identity as a Black woman. I am extremely grateful for her.

The uneasy part of going to a predominantly White school for me was being in search of my own identity. As a child, I couldn't always articulate why I felt out of place. I was surrounded by parents and siblings, but as I grew older, I realized that their understanding of God and my cultural differences was limited.

My parents simply didn't understand me and therefore didn't know how to help me navigate my emotions. They struggled with reality. This wasn't their fault. They were unconscious to who Christ really was.

They did their best. They tried to connect me to other African American families from school, and I appreciated their effort. At least they tried.

As I matured, God brought me into community with people of diverse backgrounds. Through the support of family, friends, and resources I discovered along the way, I began to piece together the broken parts of my identity.

I came to realize that being adopted had given me opportunities I might not have had otherwise. I grew up in a middle-class home that provided stability, financial security, and possibilities I wouldn't have had without my adoptive parents. I thank God for that.

For example, being able to be involved in gymnastics, dance, cooking classes, cheerleading, and attending a private school for my education were all blessings I was grateful for. We also vacationed to different states many times throughout my childhood. These experiences would allow us to broaden our perspective on life.

I was able to participate in gymnastics, dance, cooking classes, cheerleading, and attend private school. We vacationed often, and these experiences broadened our perspective on life.

Still, while providing experiences is essential to a child's growth, the most important aspect of parenting is developing a relationship with their sons and daughters. True relationship comes from relationship with Jesus and His Holy Spirit.

Most importantly we must recognize that through faith in Jesus Christ, we are all adopted into God's family and are given a new identity as children of God. He is our true Father. The word of God states:

"God decided in advance to adopt us into His own family by bringing us to Himself through Jesus Christ." —Ephesians 1:5 (NLT)

"Therefore, if anyone is in Christ, he is a new creation. The old has passed away; behold, the new has come."

—2 Corinthians 5:17 (NKJV)

Now, as an adult, I understand the importance of ensuring adopted children have support to develop and mature in a healthy manner. Genuine support derives from a relationship with Jesus. I encourage you to strengthen your relationship with Him right now. He is a right now God. If you have not given your life to Jesus, I invite you to ask Him into your heart at this very moment. He will be your God and your healer. He will heal every wound, every feeling of abandonment, rejection, and insecurity and replace it with His love, security, and assurance.

May you acknowledge that Jesus Christ is Lord over your life, and He is your Savior.

"If you confess with your mouth the Lord Jesus and believe in your heart that God has raised Him from the dead, you will be saved."—Romans 10:9 (NKJV)

Welcome to the family of Christ. Be baptized,

washed clean, and discipled. Follow the instructions in:

> *"Go therefore and make disciples of all the nations, baptizing them in the name of the Father and of the Son and of the Holy Spirit."*—Matthew 28:19 (NKJV)

Finding Cultural and Spiritual Identity in God

I have learned my identity is not solely based on my cultural background or trying to be a good person. It is rooted in being a daughter to the most high God, Jesus Christ. This understanding has truly defined my identity. Transparency and purity create a right standing with God. By following His commandments, I've come to clearly understand who I am in Him.

> *"I will be a Father to you, and you shall be My sons and daughters," says the Lord Almighty.*—2 Corinthians 6:18 (NKJV)

Though I may not have been raised by my birth father, or had the emotional guidance of my adoptive father, I have always had my Heavenly Father within me.

> *"God is within her; she will not fall; God will help her at break of day."*—Psalm 46:5 (NIV)

We give all honor and praise to our Father in Heaven. May God be glorified through this story of a young girl who fought through life, only to discover that her true identity is found in Jesus Christ.

> *"A father to the fatherless, a defender of widows, is God in His holy dwelling."*—Psalm 68:5 (NIV)

One scripture I live by and continue to pass on to my children is:

> *"When my father and my mother forsake me, then the Lord will take care of me."*—Psalm 27:10 (NKJV)

God has never failed. I know personally He has never left me and He has never forsaken me.

I pray that God comforts you and protects you as you draw near to Him, He will draw near to you. May the peace of God that surpasses all understanding come from knowing that no matter what life throws at you , you can still have joy when we know that our victory lies in Jesus Christ, and not in your own strength.

God's love is unconditional, powerful, and the most fulfilling source that you will ever encounter. May God bless you.

May God's will be done in your life.

To God be the glory forever and ever.

6

TONYA AND MIKE GENEWICK

LET GO OF THE COCONUT

It was a typical Tuesday evening, sitting around the dinner table. The kids were taking turns, well, trying, at least, with "thankful-fors;" each listing three things from the day for which they were thankful. Mike and I listened and smiled. Having spent the last few weeks in prayer and discernment, we knew it was time to get the kids' opinions.

We told them we'd been thinking of becoming foster parents. We talked about what that might mean for them, more than two of them in a bedroom (our five boys were split between three rooms), longer waits for the shower, and taking some of our focus away from them.

We explained that children in foster care sometimes come from unstable backgrounds. Perhaps just temporarily separated from their parents, perhaps victims of neglect or abuse. They might not have had food on the table, they might have suffered severe trauma. Fostering would give us an opportunity to love a child who might not know how to receive love. Or give attention to a child who is used to being ignored. Or share "thankful-fors" over dinner with a child who is used to being hungry.

About this time, our second oldest, Thomas, looked at us. His face was filled with the innocence of a child, but also the sarcasm of a teen, as he asked, so matter-of-factly, almost rhetorically, "Why wouldn't we do this?"

This mother's heart melted! The truth is, I expected Thomas to be one of the harder sells. While he can love deeply, he's fiercely protective of his family. I can't blame him, considering how he... and we, got here.

Our Beginning

Mike and I were married in June 2001, with the hopes of soon starting a family. Both Air Force officers, Mike was an A-10 pilot and I was an Aircraft Maintenance Officer, we were used to things being organized, planning for situations, and replanning when things didn't go as expected.

After almost three years of trying to start a family, and having things not go as planned, we were trying to figure out which road God wanted us to follow: further fertility treatments or adoption. We met with our priest, shared our struggles, and asked for his advice.

He told us about a man who invited a friend to go catch a monkey. They went out into the jungle with a small cage, just big enough to hold a bowl of shredded coconut. The friend didn't see how they could possibly catch a monkey with such a small cage but was assured he just needed to wait and watch. After a while, a monkey came along, put his hand through a small hole in the cage, and then grabbed a handful of coconut. With his hand now in a fist, the monkey couldn't get it back out of the hole, no matter how hard he pulled. He kept trying and trying, but his fist wouldn't fit through the hole. He was stuck! If he dropped the coconut, he could get his hand out. But he wouldn't. He couldn't. He could be free if he would just let go of the coconut. Father looked at us and offered his advice: *let go of the coconut!*

God was calling us to something we had talked about since we first started dating: adoption.

> *"Do not be afraid; from now on you will be catching men."*—Luke 5:10

Thus began a journey that would last almost nine years. Over those years, we would meet with twelve birth mothers, be selected by eleven , have five change their mind before placement, hold seven babies in our arms, bring six babies into our home, and actually adopt five baby boys. It was a roller coaster filled with countless highs and lows, but one we would choose to ride again, despite the tears, for the sake of our boys.

Our Boys

Joseph: In late April 2004, we started our adoption journey. We had to make a lot of choices. Would we accept a baby with drug exposure? Would we accept a baby with health issues? Would we accept a mixed-race baby? Which races? Our initial answer to all of those questions was, quite simply, "Yes, we don't care!" But after a little more discussion, we realized we had one concern.

We were concerned that if we adopted a black baby, we would face *criticism* and *pressure* to raise him or her a certain way. This broke our hearts, but it led us to say we would consider adopting a baby of any racial mix other than black.

One week after we were officially eligible to adopt, we got a phone call telling us there was a five-month-old Hispanic baby boy, named José who would be available the following day. The birth parents had chosen us specifically, because we are Catholic, like them. Were we interested? YES!!

We went shopping—nine months of shopping in about 3 hours. The birth mom wanted to meet us, but the agency didn't want us there when she arrived. They asked us to wait at a nearby restaurant until they called. The agency kept checking in with us, but the birth mother wasn't showing and always had a different excuse. After seven and a half hours, they finally told us to go home. If they heard anything, they would call. We went home and prayed—a lot! Over the weekend, there was still no news. We finally put everything away, took the car seat out of the car, and tried to return to a normal life.

Monday, I submitted my six-month notice to separate from the Air Force. Two weeks later, I went to work as usual. This particular Monday, I had to travel out of town. I was two hours from home and three hours from the agency. I got a call at 1:50 pm, asking if we were ready to come pick up our son. The paperwork was signed, and he was waiting for us!

I called Mike, who was literally four minutes away from stepping out to the flight-line for a two-hour mission. I asked how he felt about not flying that day, because we had a baby. He was able to find someone else to take his flight, and we met at home, then headed to the agency and met our son! On October 18, 2004, Joseph was born into our hearts. We chose his name to honor both his birth parents and Jesus' adoptive father. Joseph was a happy healthy baby.

> *Whoever receives one child such as this in my name, receives me; and whoever receives me, receives not me but the One who sent me."*—Mark 9:37

Joseph was actually born on April 27, 2004, right when we began working with the agency, but we weren't ready for him then. God is good.

Shortly after bringing Joseph home, a family member, upon learning he was Hispanic, asked if we were going to raise him *with his culture*. Wow. We weren't expecting that. We had avoided adopting a black baby, to avoid that pressure. We hadn't prepared for that pressure with a Hispanic baby. This led us to reevaluate our adoption plans and our parenting philosophy. After much discussion and even more prayer, we decided that more important than raising our son Hispanic was raising him Catholic. With a foundational love of Christ, strong morals, Godly values, and a fundamental respect for all lives, raising our children in our faith was more important than anything else. We also realized that this focus could be applied to any child, regardless of their skin color or national origin.

Thomas: After moving, in September 2005, we began working with a new adoption agency. This time we had no restrictions on anything. In January 2006, we were matched with a birth mother who was expecting a baby boy. On Tuesday, February 14, a little *girl* was born. She was biracial, Hispanic and Black, and she was beautiful!! It was so special for us to be there when she was born. We will never forget it!

Two days later, when it was time to be released from the hospital, the birth mom told us she needed to say goodbye to the baby away from the hospital. She looked us in the eye, insisted we had nothing to worry about; we were her parents, and we believed her. We all left the hospital at about 1 p.m. The social worker was supposed to pick up the baby around 8 p.m. and bring her to us. But at 8:30 p.m. the social worker called us to say she couldn't find the birth mother anywhere. She looked everywhere she could and called everyone she could until almost midnight. The next day, three separate times the birth mother was supposed to go to the agency with the baby to sign papers, but she always had an excuse and didn't show. By 2 p.m., she was unreachable. That continue all weekend. On Monday morning the agency finally found her and she *finally* admitted she was keeping the baby. We cried for days.

Five weeks later the birth mother called us and told us she changed her mind and wanted us to have the baby. After much discussion, meeting with her, and working through the details, everything was set. She was going to get the baby and meet us back at the lawyer's office in one hour. We never saw or heard from her again. Again, we cried for days. We have no idea why she came back, only to leave again. We have no idea why we had to experience the heart-break a second time.

> *"I consider that the sufferings of this present time are as nothing compared with the glory to be revealed for us."*
>
> —Romans 8:18

Sometime after that, I said to Mike, "I know God has a plan for everything, but I'd sure like to know what His plan was here." Mike reminded me, maybe it's not about us, maybe it's about that baby girl. Based on what we know of her birth mother, she is probably going to have a rough life, but she will always be our first little girl. We pray for her daily, as we pray for all our children. We believe that God brought her to us, and us to her, so we could meet her, hold her, love her, and pray for her. God is good.

A few months later, on our fifth wedding anniversary, in June 2006, we met Marie, who was expecting a baby boy in early September. This relationship was comfortable from the beginning. No roller coaster, no struggles and wonderful conversations. We went with her to prenatal appointments. Everything was moving along wonderfully, then in mid-July, we found out I was pregnant. We talked about whether we should call off the adoption, but like each time before, I lost the baby by six weeks.

We continued the path that was set in motion. On August 13, I stood by Marie's side as she gave birth to Thomas. She named him Paul Thomas but told us we could name him whatever we wanted. We thought Thomas was a beautiful name! He is biracial, White and Black, with the most amazing head of curls and a smile that contains just enough mischief to make any parent worry. He was a happy and healthy baby, although time would reveal learning disabilities and autism, as well as some genetic mental health conditions.. We have an incredible open adoption with Marie. Although she lives in another state, we talk often and keep in touch through social media. God is good.

Gabriel: In 2008, we were ready for number three. We met with a birth mom in July, who chose a different family for her baby. We met another birth mom in October, against the recommendation of the agency—they didn't think she was serious about placing. But we had come to realize it wasn't about placing. We wanted to meet her, show her the love of Christ, and help her figure out what is best, whatever that might be. She decided she wanted to place her baby with us. We went to an appointment on October 30, the doctor said the birth mother and baby were healthy and almost ready for delivery. When we went back the following week, she didn't show. The doctor's office couldn't tell us anything, but they did call the agency to tell them she had delivered the baby on October 31. She had changed her mind about placing her baby for adoption. We didn't cry this time.We trusted God's plan. We were matched again in March, but after a few weeks, and a lot of pressure from her family, that birth mother also changed her mind.

> *"Therefore, since we have been justified by faith, we have peace with God through our Lord Jesus Christ. Not only that, but we even boast of our afflictions, knowing that affliction produces endurance, and endurance, proven character, and proven character, hope."*—
> Romans 5:1, 3–4

In late May 2009, we were visiting Disney World with friends. On a Thursday, while standing in line for the Toy Story ride, we received a phone call from the agency. They had a birth mom who was due in two weeks and wanted to meet us, they asked, "when would we be home?" We told them we'd be home on Tuesday. The next day they called again, the birth mother had been to the doctor, was dilated to 2 cm, and could deliver any day. They asked if we could come home sooner. We left Saturday as planned, the following day, but made the trip in two days instead of four. Sunday morning, in the hotel, Mike's phone alerted him, as it often did, to the particular saint's or celebratory feast day for that day. It was the Feast of the Visitation. Mike looked at me, with a very serious face and declared, "If this baby is a girl, and she's born today, we *WILL* name her Mary Elizabeth." I knew what he meant, and yet, I made the "mistake" of questioning him. "Was the Visitation when Mary visited Elizabeth, or when the angel Gabriel visited Mary? Oh, never mind, Gabriel visiting Mary is the Annunciation. But since we're discussing it, if it's a boy and he's born today, I don't necessarily want to name him John. But I do like Gabriel." Mike agreed that he also liked Gabriel.

We met Nicole the next day. It was a great match from the beginning. Conversation was easy and open. She asked us how we had chosen the names of our other children, and we told her we picked strong Christian names which also honored their birth parents. She told us we could name this baby whatever we wanted, but ever since she found out she was having a boy, she'd been calling him Gabriel. Gabriel! The following Sunday we got the call that she was in labor. Just after 3 a.m., we were blessed with Gabriel. At birth, he tested positive for alcohol and marijuana. We also know he had prenatal exposure to methamphetamines. Years later, he was diagnosed with Fetal Alcohol Syndrome, which affects his physical features and his central nervous system. He is also autistic, has mild learning disabilities, and has dysgraphia. But he is truly one of the happiest people, with the most amazing sense of humor we have ever met! While he is one quarter Cuban, his fair skin and light hair actually made me blend into the family a little bit, as Mike's Italian heritage gave him olive skin and dark brown hair.

Most people thought we were crazy for adopting another baby right then. Mike was getting out of the Air Force in less than a month and didn't have a job waiting. I had been praying for God to be a cloud to us as He was to the Israelites and lead us where he wanted us. This is where He led us! Seven hours after Gabriel's birth, Mike received the job offer he'd been praying for!

"I am Gabriel, God's servant, and I was sent to tell you this good news."—Luke 1:19

We finalized Gabriel's adoption in December. That same day, before we even left the courthouse, the agency told us they had a "perfect" match for us. They usually require 18 months between placements but were going to make an exception. The birth mother was expecting a little girl in February. She was raised with lots of older brothers and wanted the same for her daughter. We met and everything seemed amazing. On February 10, Rebekah was born. She was fully Black, with a head full of curls and the chubbiest cheeks. Her birth mother didn't want to spend much time with her. "Beka" was having a tough time regulating temperature, so she spent a lot of time in the nursery under warming lights. I was by her side every minute!

We were ready to take her home l before the birth mom could legally sign relinquishment papers, but she could release the baby to the agency who then released her to us. We finally brought home our baby girl and introduced her to her big brothers! The next day, Saturday February 13, the agency called us to tell us the birth mother was refusing to sign. We had to return Beka. I felt like my heart was ripped from my chest. The following day, February 14, was our first Baby Girl's fourth birthday. We cried, and cried, and cried. We kept reminding ourselves, God has a plan, God is good… and then we cried some more.

JohnPaul: In 2011, when we decided we were ready again, our agency had a waiting list of adoptive families. So, we found ourselves looking for new options. On March 29, I called Catholic Charities. The woman on the phone asked what we were looking for, to which I replied "A baby" but knew what she meant. I explained our previous adoptions, the various race combinations of our children, as well as the drug exposures we knew about. I explained how we acknowledge that a lot of women don't realize they are pregnant until close to the end of the first trimester. Even a birth mother with the best of intentions might still drink or smoke until she knows she is pregnant, so we have no restrictions on drug and alcohol exposure. Further, we believe that if I did carry a healthy pregnancy to term, our baby could still have complications like Down's Syndrome, cleft lip, or heart disease. We take each situation presented to us and pray about it.

She told us they did not have a waiting family that was as accepting of the many "variables" as I had just described. They sent us an application and we got started. We called back on April 15 to ask a couple of questions, and they wanted to know how long it was going to take us to complete the required home study; they had a two-week-old baby boy, who needed a family. He was born addicted to crack (cocaine) but seemed to be doing ok.

> *"Pure and genuine religion in the sight of God the Father means caring for orphans and widows in their distress."*—James 1:27

Our original agency, who handled our home study, came over the next morning. We worked like crazy over the weekend finishing our application. The following week was Holy Week; we spent a lot of time in prayer. When we called a few days after Easter to make sure they had received all our paperwork, we also asked what would happen if the birth mother didn't choose one of the profiles shown to her. In a case like that, they would choose the most compatible family that had been waiting the longest. Obviously, that wouldn't be us. Later that week they called back. The birth mother had stopped returning phone calls, they didn't know where she was, but a decision needed to be made, because this baby deserved a home. They chose us! Unfortunately, the family caring for him had taken a weekend trip, so we couldn't meet him until Tuesday. It was Divine Mercy Sunday. We spent that weekend watching the Beatification of Blessed John Paul II, on TV. On Tuesday May 3, we were blessed with our fourth son, JohnPaul, an absolutely gorgeous, almost bald baby boy who is a perfect combination of Hispanic, White, and Black. He was born on March 31, two days after we first called Catholic Charities. Despite his early addiction, JohnPaul is ridiculously smart and is a very talented athlete. God is good.

Jacob: About 18 months later, we called Catholic Charities, again. While we'd never had any limitations on gender, this time we asked for a girl. Within a month, they called us to say they had a "perfect" match (adoption agencies use this term a lot!), *except* the birth mother was expecting a boy. We laughed. We prayed. I was ready to say yes, but I tend to react with emotions. So, I specifically prayed that God would help me to be an "Ephesians 5 wife," to trust my husband, as head of our home, to make a decision that was best for our family. He prayed for God to lead him to the right decision. Ultimately, we decided to trust God. Maybe we weren't meant to have a daughter. Several meetings and a few appointments later, everything with the birth mother was on track. Then Catholic Charities called to tell us they found out the birth mother had gone to the hospital, delivered the baby, and left the hospital with the baby. Apparently, she'd also been working with two other adoption agencies and had no intention of placing her baby for adoption.. Our hearts were broken, but not like before. We knew God was in control. Two weeks later, Catholic Charities called to check on us. They told us they heard from JohnPaul's birth mother, whom we had never met, not for lack of trying.

She wanted to meet us.

She was in labor with another boy.

She wanted the brothers to be together.

Twelve hours later we met JohnPaul's younger brother. He had a head full of black curls, but otherwise looked just like JohnPaul, but also completely different! As Mike sat in the nursery at the hospital, rocking this tiny little baby, I was watching through the window, as they would only allow one of us at a time inside the nursery, admiring what an amazing husband I had and thanking God for His blessings. My phone buzzed; Mike texted me:

> *"And after that came forth his brother, and his hand had hold of his heel; and his name was called Jacob."*—Genesis 25:25

Jacob was prenatally exposed to the same drugs that JohnPaul had been but showed no signs of addiction when he was born. Years later, Jacob was diagnosed with dyslexia, but just like so many *youngest* children, he doesn't let anything slow him down, including dyslexia. God is good.

Eye Opening Race Issues

We love all our children, regardless of their skin color or racial origin. We thought that was enough. Then we realized how much race plays into even the little things. Our children attended a private school that wished to take a survey of demographics. We struggled to complete the survey. We had no concerns about sharing our children's racial details, but we were deeply concerned about how the school would use that information. Yes, we had two children who were Hispanic or part Hispanic, one child who was part Black, and two children who were part Black and part Hispanic. But *WE* are not a Hispanic family. *WE* are not a Black family. *WE* are not a White family. *WE* don't fit in a box on a piece of paper.

We lived outside the city and our kids transferred to the small rural public school. A school that, as it turns out, was almost entirely White. The first week of school, a friend overheard another kindergarten mom say, "I can't believe they put my daughter in class with that little Black boy!" She was referring to JohnPaul. We were shocked. Joseph was told to "hurry up and jump a fence before Trump builds a wall and doesn't let you in!" Again, shocked.

The following year we moved to a larger city nearby, and our children three in elementary, one in middle school, and one in high school transferred to the city schools. They all went to very diverse schools. For the first time, each of them had friends in class who looked like them.

We came to the very sudden and very harsh understanding that maybe we had made mistakes. Of course, loving our children was vital. Teaching them to love Jesus was non-negotiable. Instilling in them a strong moral foundation and a love for all people was unquestionably the right thing to do. But ignoring their skin color had been a mistake. We love our children, and their racial backgrounds don't change that. But we had never really acknowledged that the mere color of their skin could make *other* people treat them differently. We hadn't understood their need to be around people who looked like them. We hadn't understood their desire to see their physical traits reflected in the shows they watch. We realized it was time to have some big conversations with our kids. Actually, it was long past time!

Changes

We'd always enjoyed watching tv as a family. Any given evening in our home will probably find us watching old reruns of *Friends* or *The Big Bang Theory*. Our kids all know and love these shows, but we decided maybe we should try something new for them. We introduced them to *The Fresh Prince of Bel*

Air, Family Matters, Everybody Hates Chris, and for the older boys, *Martin.* They loved these new shows, too!

We found people who had hair like the kids to cut the kids' hair. We stepped away from our comfort zone of short, clean-cut styles and let the boys experiment and express themselves with their hair. I even tried my hand at twists and braids, though I admit it's not my strongest skill.

We also had some hard conversations with our kids, especially the teens. We hated telling them that they can't act the same way as their friends. If they are ever at a party, and the cops show up, they *CAN'T* run, even if their White friends run. They aren't White, and unfortunately, won't be treated the same. If their White friends talk back to adults or police officers, that doesn't mean they can also talk back. It is vitally important that they always speak with the respect and manners they've been taught, regardless of what their friends do, because failure to do so could result in much worse consequences, simply because of the color of their skin. That's a heart-breaking and gut-wrenching conversation to have with your kids, but we realized it was necessary. Unfortunately, there are just too many people in this world who see skin color first and pass judgement based on what they see.

As we continued watching our kids grow and navigate these challenges, we wondered how many children might not have parents willing to have these hard conversations with them or any conversations at all. We wondered how many children might not have parents… or a home, or a bed, or healthy food, or a safe place… and we wondered if we might be able to help. We began praying, asking for God's guidance. Once again, we were trying to figure out which road God wanted us to follow, more adoption or foster care.

We reached out to a local child placing agency within the foster system. We went to an informational meeting. We continued to pray. And then, we found ourselves sitting around the dinner table, on that typical Tuesday evening with Thomas asking his rhetorical question, "Why wouldn't we do this?" Why, indeed! Knowing our kids were on board for this next step in our journey removed any remaining questions.

Fostering

As we went through the foster licensing process, we had to fill out checklists indicating what "variables" we would accept with a placement. These options ranged from race, gender, and age to drug exposure, medical issues, and behavioral issues. The answers to these questions were easy for us.

We'd already experienced such a vast array of "variables" in our boys, we knew we were prepared to face anything God brought our way. We did have one restriction: we wanted our boys' birth order to remain intact, so we only wanted a child aged six or younger, and that age increased as Jacob aged.

We welcomed our first foster child in May of 2020. What a wild time to jump into this new journey! She needed quite a variety of therapies: speech therapy, occupational therapy, & physical therapy. Navigating all these appointments and agency visits during COVID lockdowns was extremely challenging, but it was a joy to have her in our family. She was with us for almost a year. We also provided respite care to a few other children, when their foster families needed a little help. We knew we were doing the work God needed us to do.

MaryElizabeth. In June 2021, we welcomed a baby girl into our home, MaryElizabeth, and our world was flipped upside down. She'd been born prematurely, with alcohol and methamphetamines in her system. Weighing a tiny 2 lbs 14oz, at birth, she was less than 12 lbs at seven months when she came to us. She was behind in basic milestones, but otherwise seemed healthy. A beautiful mixed race little girl. All that work Tonya had done learning to braid hair was really going to get put to use!

Very soon after MaryElizabeth arrived, we all realized this was not going to be a *typical* foster placement. There was just something about this little girl. Unfortunately, her biological parents weren't in a position to care for her and wouldn't be for many years. Her biological grandmother was raising two of her siblings and we had frequent visits with them. At our house, during her first birthday celebration, her grandma asked if we would be willing to adopt her. Wow! Adoption was never in our plan for this chapter of life. But God was at work, and we soon realized she was going to become a permanent part of our family. Eighteen months after she arrived, we finalized her adoption. As she grew, her delays became more noticeable. She didn't walk until almost 21 months, and she didn't start talking until after that. She received speech, occupational, and physical therapies multiple times each week. Then, almost as if to reinforce the fact that she works on her timeline and hers alone, the month before she turned three, she graduated from all three therapies, as she was ahead of her age level across the board. God is so good!

David: Oh, David! When we became foster parents, we had no intention of adopting, again. This was supposed to be a different journey. MaryElizabeth just had a plan of her own. Joseph graduated high school in 2022. At about that same time, we knew for sure we would be adopting MaryElizabeth. Someone asked us if we were done. YES! MaryElizabeth would definitely be our last adoption. We would keep our foster license, but our family was complete. We moved Joseph to college on July 30, 2022. On July 31, 2022, a little boy was born who needed a home. He tested positive for alcohol, amphetamines, and methamphetamines at birth. We were asked to take care of him. We laughed and cried. God has quite a sense of humor. We talked about all the reasons this was crazy. We asked. "Why wouldn't we do this?" After much prayer, we agreed, there was no reason to say no. So David joined our home. A fragile baby, with breathing difficulties and vision issues, physical and speech delays, he is also a perfect mix of Black, White, and Hispanic. We've been asked by both friends and strangers if he and JohnPaul are related, because they look so much alike. We believe that is just another way God is telling us He is in control. David came to us a foster, but God's plans are bigger than ours. His birth mother was not able to care for him. His birth father has serious health issues and struggles to care for himself. So, David remained with us for two years and ten months, before finally becoming a permanent family member! God is so very good!

What's Next

When we began our journey, we were concerned other people would tell us how to parent. We thought we could avoid that by avoiding certain variables. We quickly learned that some people would tell you how to parent, regardless! But it doesn't matter. They are free to parent their children as they wish. We will parent ours as we see fit. We still believe that instilling a foundational love of Christ, along with strong morals, Godly values, and a fundamental respect for all lives, is essential, but it's not enough. Acknowledging our children's physical traits, their mental gifts and limitations, their background, and their heritage is also important. Introducing them to people that look like them, watching tv shows, listening to music, and choosing hairstyles that help them express themselves, is also important. If we could go back and change the way we parented when our oldest kids were younger, would we? Maybe. But I think lots of parents might say yes to that, simply because time and experience bring wisdom. Will we likely parent MaryElizabeth & David a little differently than the older boys? Probably. Will we still need to have those hard conversations, reminding them that they are not the same as their White friends? Unfortunately, yes. Do we hope that all our children always know how much we love them and that, while they know we aren't perfect, and we know we aren't perfect, we did the best we could, with what we knew? Absolutely!

If you've ever wondered if you could or should adopt a child of another race, we would offer you this advice: Let go of your concerns. Let go of your worries. Let go of your vision of perfection. Just let go of the coconut!

Blurred Edges

Adoption blurs the edges
between miracles, where boldly
painted strokes scrawl
across a sea of dotted lines.

Signatures crisscross documents
like fingertips reaching small hands,
revealing open hearts teemed
with stories stitched up tight.

But there—see it now!
Tiny red threads, loose along the fray,
await to weave exuberance
and reverie with another soul.

Those with courage, willing
to immerse and etch their hearts
far beyond ethnicity or expectation
scrawled along dotted lines—

and blurred edges.

~Celaine Charles

Have a Story to Share?
We're gathering stories for the next
Beyond Skin Deep book.

CoachPearl@gmail.com
813-449-3308
WSLiving.com

Let your voice be part of the journey.

Made in the USA
Columbia, SC
10 August 2025

61288191R00050